MASTERFUL MESSAGING

VOLUME 1

COMPELLING COPY

HARNESSING THE POWER OF WORDS

GAIL DIXON

Parker House Publishing
ParkerHouseBooks.com

Book design: Candi Parker
Editing: Judee Light
Published by ParkerHouseBooks.com

What people are saying...

"In this brilliant book Gail Dixon has provided a roadmap for Masterful Messaging. Whether you're writing sales copy, creating a presentation or wanting to connect in a more authentic and influential manner, this book has it all! Gail's gift as a word wizard is more evident than ever as she guides us through the process of harnessing the power of our words to create clear, concise and compelling communication."

~ Nancy Matthews, International Speaker, Best Selling Author & Co-Founder of Women's Prosperity Network

"After all these years in management, teaching and consulting, I thought I had a great handle on messaging and communication. After reading Gail's book, I am making notes like crazy to help improve my writing and communication. Great practical knowledge and tips to increase the 'oomph' of your writing. Thank you, Gail."

~ John Jorgensen SPHR, SHRM-SCP, Strategic Advisor, Illinois State Council of SHRM

"Gail has a gift with words that is rare and precious. Her phrases are like strings of gems carefully laid out for our delight and understanding, each one making its mark and lighting the way home."

~ Licia Berry, Best Selling Author, Speaker, Mentor, Leader

"Gail Dixon's new book, *Masterful Messaging, Volume 1,* 'had me at Hello' and kept me right through to 'Happy writing.' It's a tiny book packed with commanding content and generous gems of wisdom. Beautifully written, every word persuades the reader that you are in the presence of a master. And you are. I can't wait for *Volume 2!*"

> ~ *Kathryn A. Hathaway, Esq., Chief Phoenix, Being the Phoenix*

"Copywriting and messaging expert Gail Dixon takes you briskly through the must-do points of constructing attention-getting, persuasive copy. I found myself wishing every educational book was written this way, specific, short, sweet and direct. Follow her outline and you WILL accomplish 80% of the task as promised!

Among the best pieces to check out: the customer thoughts checklist, how to test your titles, how to cement your impact with subtitles, the secrets of hidden conversation, and my personal passion, Conversation Marketing. Gail writes the way you want to learn to write - for maximum impact and with clarity. A must have in every business person's library, and maybe the next Strunk and White."

> ~ *Deanna A Mims, MarketDone, Marketing and Business Development*

Dedication

This book is dedicated to the memory of
my grandfather, George Kelsall, who taught me
to love words and to understand their power.

Acknowledgements

In this project, as in every important experience in my life, I have been fortunate to have many people providing encouragement, advice and support. I am grateful for my siblings who have been cheering for me behind the scenes in every job I ever had, and for friends who waited patiently through many years of exploring possibilities until Masterful Messaging came into being – especially Audrey, Charlotte, Kay, and Kris.

In more recent days, the Women's Prosperity Network community has provided the coaching, training and support that pushed me from ideas into action. I am thankful for my connection to this group. I am also grateful to Fabienne Fredrickson of the Client Attraction Business School for issuing the challenge to write the book and to my fellow CABS students who have been companions on the journey.

Gina Hogan Edwards, Writing and Creativity Coach offered just the right combination of prodding and offering space to get me into the rhythm of writing again. Candi Parker of Parker House Publishing and Judee Light, Editor Extraordinaire, worked wonders with tight deadlines to make my manuscript into this book.

Finally, I am thankful for my god daughter, Janie, whose love and laughter light my days.

Masterful Messaging

About This Series

If you are content with close enough in your business and your life, read no further. This series of books is not meant for you. On the other hand, if you want to be sure that you are meeting or exceeding your goals, making deep and lasting connections with others, and creating the life of your dreams, then you will want to become a master at messaging. This series of books about the power of words – in business and in life – was created just for you! Each book in the series explores what it takes to become masterful at a particular type of messaging. We'll look at the components of each type of message, break down the steps to creating a masterful message and offer tips on what works and what doesn't.

These books are small, practical, hands-on guides to masterful messaging. They do not contain complicated research, academic jargon or abstract theory. Nor are they full of pushy sales hype designed to get you to spend thousands of dollars on a specific product or program. I am not promising you a no-fail way to win the lottery or become the next Nobel Prize winner. What I AM offering is the wisdom I have learned from hundreds of messaging masters condensed into clear, easy-to-follow guides to creating your own masterful messages.

Volume 1: Compelling Copy

This book, Volume 1, is focused on masterful messaging for business through compelling sales copy. Here's a little preview. First, we discuss the definition of masterful messaging and explore what makes a message masterful. Then, we talk about why great copy is such an important tool to propel your business forward – and provide seven keys to supercharging your copy so that it consistently fuels your sales success.

We move on to talk about headlines and how to master the skill of writing headlines that capture attention every time. Next, we explore how to use copy to state your unique brand value and the ways that you can set yourself apart from the crowd. Finally, we describe the four parts of an irresistible call to action – the switch that turns people from browsers into buyers.

Once you learn to create compelling copy, with practice you'll become a messaging master and then the sky's the limit. Let's get started!

TABLE OF CONTENTS

Introduction

For as long as I can remember, I have been fascinated with the power of words. My mother told me that I started talking at nine months old and that I didn't know when to stop. She was right – my otherwise good report cards often carried a bad mark for "talking in class." It didn't take much imagination to figure out that when people referred to me and my sisters, it would be, "Lori is the singer, Cheryl is the dancer and Gail is the talker."

When it was time to choose a career, I became a speech and French teacher and a lifelong student of communication. The wonderful nuances of the French language sent me searching for similar gems in English. When I found those gems, they came in multiple syllables and I used every one of them! My circle of friends and colleagues sometimes welcomed it and sometimes winced when I relied on my extensive vocabulary to make a point. Often as not, my wording was a ten-pound rock in a five-pound sack – pretty, but probably twice as much as necessary. My grown-up professional self is still in love with words.

I am still learning about the power of words, recognizing that words describe, define and sometimes even determine our reality. A well-placed word often makes the difference between yes and no, between right and wrong, between good and bad, between love and hate.

Here's what I know – people who are masters at messaging are masters at life. Every interaction we have with others – individually or in groups, in person or over the airwaves – is a series of messages sent and received. People who do it well, on both the sending and the receiving end, are able to create the connections and circumstances that move them forward in positive directions.

So, why doesn't everybody work to possess the power of masterful messaging? First, just as with any skill, it takes time and effort to become a true master at messaging. Second, for many people masterful messaging is not seen as an essential life skill. Once we acquire language, many of us are content to make do with average or above average communication skills. Close enough is often good enough. If we are lucky, others fill in the blank when we search for just the right word, forgive us when we falter or teach us when necessary. And, when words don't work, we have other tools – time, money, power – to get the job done. At least that's what we tell ourselves. But nothing could be further from the truth.

In reality, masterful messaging is a potent tool for boosting results in business and in life. Delivering the right message to the right person in the right way can create maximum impact and yield powerful results. Nowhere is this more evident than in the world of sales. It's not enough to have the best product or service – people need to *know* that your product or service is the best. Your bottom line is directly proportional to how well you convey your value to your potential customers. This book provides specific guidelines on how to create compelling copy to superpower your sales success. It's time to enter the world of masterful messaging!

"The key is to write it so that they hear it and it slides through the brain and goes straight to the heart."
~ *Maya Angelou*

Chapter One

What Is Masterful Messaging?

You were born communicating. From the first cry you make to announce your entry into this world until the last breath you take, you are sending messages about yourself, others and the world around you. In those early days and years, your messages were largely reactive and instinctive rather than deliberate and intentional. Even so, they got the job done. Your parents or caregivers recognized that you needed attention and they even began to distinguish between hungry, wet, tired, angry, and frightened cries.

Once you acquire the magic of language, your communication becomes more intentional. You use your messages to make connections with other people and to describe and define your experience. Through repetition and mimicry, you learn that sounds come together to form words and that words have meaning. Eventually, you string words together to convey your thoughts, emotions and intentions to others. It's magical. What you recognize and envision in your mind comes out in code that other people receive and understand. The more skilled you become with words, the more successful you can be in life.

What Makes a Message Masterful?

So how can you harness the power of words to create masterful messaging? First, let's take a look at what makes a message masterful. The first essential quality of a masterful message is authenticity. Authentic messages represent the true intention, feelings and beliefs of the sender without any desire to mislead or manipulate the message recipient. Masterful messages also meet the criteria outlined by Scott M. Cutlip in his book *Effective Public Relations* (1953).

#1 Completeness

Masterful messages contain all of the essential information that allows your recipient to understand your intention and respond appropriately.

#2 Conciseness

Being concise is not about keeping the message short, but rather about keeping it focused on the key point you are trying to convey without redundant or irrelevant information.

#3 Consideration

Masterful communicators consider and value the needs, moods and points of view of the recipients of their messages.

#4 Concreteness

Effective communication happens when the message is timely, consistent, and supported by evidence such as statistics and examples.

#5 Courtesy

Courtesy is the first cousin to consideration. Courtesy means being respectful of your audience's culture, values and beliefs and taking care that the message is created in a way that people can easily relate to and understand.

#6 Clarity

Clear messages are focused on a single objective and they use words that are easily understood by the audience.

#7 Correctness

Using grammar and syntax correctly is essential for masterful messaging. The correct use of language avoids misunderstandings and establishes the credibility of the person sending the message.

What Masterful Communicators Know

In any field, masters are those who have highly developed knowledge and skills that set them apart from others. So what is it that masterful communicators know that others do not? L. Michael Hall, a leading practitioner of Neuro-linguistic Programming (NLP), suggests that masterful communicators have some powerful skills that enable them to craft their messages so that they are most effective. These skills include:

- Sensory awareness – an ability to take in the maximum amount of information from your five senses and make sense of that information.

- Being present in the moment – the ability to focus on the now, to express and react in the current conversation or interaction, rather than re-experiencing the past or anticipating the future.

- Observing objectively – the ability to recognize that your experience is not the only possible experience.

- Valuing the receiver of your message as much as you value yourself.

- Staying open and receptive to feedback – understanding the messaging process is a shared experience and that communication flows in two directions.

- Remaining flexible – being willing to adjust to real-time feedback and make on-course corrections.

- Thinking systemically and applying leverage – understanding the points where influence and adjustment can be applied to direct the interaction toward its intended outcome.

- Exploring curiously to discover what is – an ability to remain open to new experiences and interpretations.

- Seeking clarity in problem-definition – working consistently to eliminate ambiguity or misunderstanding.

- Focusing on solutions – removing barriers to successful communication and facilitating forward momentum. (adapted from *Communication Magic*, 2002)

Masterful utilization of these skills will maximize the effectiveness of the messages you send and increase the likelihood that your messages will create the results that you intend.

Becoming a Message Master

While it could take a lifetime to describe every possible tweak or tip that you can use to make your message masterful, there are some basic concepts that can serve as guidelines regardless of the context in which your message will be sent. (adapted from David Portney, *7 Secrets of Master Communicators*)

First – Start with a clear result in mind. Getting the intended outcome from your message is taking a journey from here to there. Just as with any other journey, you have to know where you are going in order to be sure to get there. Create a clear picture in your mind of what you want your audience to do, think, say or feel as a result of your message. Master messengers have a clear vision of what they want to achieve through their message.

Second – Act immediately and decisively. Once you have your clear result in mind, communicate immediately to the person or people you are trying to influence or persuade. Take only the time you need to make sure you have considered your audience and crafted your message in a way that they can best respond – and then deliver the message! There is only one guarantee in the world of communication – 100% of the messages you *don't* send will fail to get you what you want.

Third – Be aware of results and responses along the way. Communication masters pay close attention to the results and feedback they are getting from their audiences. Encourage feedback from others and assess the results of your communication by listening to the responses you get. Don't just listen, also watch very carefully when you are speaking face to face. Then pay close attention to the nonverbal responses you get. Remember that only about 7% of communication is verbal. Pay attention to that other 93% and adjust accordingly. Nonverbal cues include tone of voice, facial expressions, body postures, and gestures that go along with the verbal response.

Fourth – Stay flexible and be willing to adjust. The message you intend may not necessarily be the message your audience receives. By paying attention to verbal and nonverbal feedback, you will know when the response you are getting is different than the clear picture you had in mind from the very beginning. If you are getting a response different than what you wanted, immediately adjust your communication accordingly. As the message creator, you are fully responsible for ensuring that your message meets the mark.

Fifth – Operate from a place of authenticity and excellence. Your message will be most masterful when you create it from a clear and positive state of mind. Communicate your message with purpose, passion and power. When your energy is contagious, your ability to inspire, influence and motivate others is heightened. Your positive state of mind can influence your audience and move them in the direction that you intend.

Sixth – Recognize and respond to resistance. Master communicators work to achieve rapport with others. Resistance to your message means that rapport is missing. Establishing rapport begins even before you create your message. Understanding your audience and what motivates them will help you to craft a message that connects. If you experience resistance, it means that there is not enough rapport and affinity with your target audience. Never blame your audience for being resistant to your message. When you encounter resistance, work at building greater rapport.

Seventh – Learn how to deliver your message effectively. Even the best-crafted message can fall short if it is not delivered effectively. Messaging masters are not born, they are made. Utilizing the best channels for message delivery and the best techniques for speaking or writing will maximize the effectiveness of your message. If you want to get results, achieve your goals and make your dreams come true, take charge of your communication.

Learn how to conquer fear and master your state of mind. Become an expert at creating rapport and affinity with others. Become proficient at directing your face, voice tone, body posture, and gestures. When you can persuade and motivate with personal power and precision, you position yourself for success.

Chapter Two

Compelling Copy: Your Sales Super Power

Have you ever wished you had a super power that could boost your business success? Effective sales copy is exactly that – it's the key to making sure that you connect with your ideal customers not just on the surface, but on a deeper level that keeps them coming back.

It feels like magic when you and your customer "click" with each other – they are getting their needs met and you are fulfilling your mission, being of service AND getting well-compensated for your work. Effective sales copy is the super power that makes the magic happen! With effective sales copy, there should be no doubt in your customers' minds that you understand their needs, that you can solve their problems, and that they need to buy from you.

So...why am I writing this book? After all, I am a copy writer. Do you wonder if maybe I am putting myself out of business? The truth is there is so much business and sales communication going on in the world every day that I could work around the clock and not make a dent in it. Every copy writer in existence could work around the clock – and we

STILL wouldn't make a dent in it. And then of course, there's the question of who could possibly afford to have every bit of their business communication copy written for them. Nobody! That's who!

Every time you talk about your business – in informal networking or cocktail party chit-chat, on your web site, in your ads, in your publications – it's all sales copy. I suspect many of you reading this book may have a bit of an aversion to the word "sales" – it brings up images of that used car salesman who shouts at you from the television – or the pushy guy who won't take no for an answer. I know you don't want to be like them!

And I don't want you to! So, just for now, maybe we can think of sales copy as persuasive speech or using words to influence action. Okay? Feel better? Great! So......let's go!

3 Cs of Compelling Copy

Powerful copy meets three basic standards – it is clear, concise and compelling. Let's take a minute to explore what we mean by each of these terms.

Clear	Concise	Compelling

CLEAR

Be able to describe to your potential customers how they will feel when they are satisfied users of your product or service. What does it look like when their needs are met and their problems solved?

Make it clear!
Clear copy is simple, straightforward and selective.

Simple - You've all probably heard the rule of thumb that the average American adult reads at a 7th-grade level. Yep. It turns out, if you want to communicate effectively to an American adult, you should pretend they have the reading level of a 12-year-old. So – don't use a $10 word when a $2 one will work just as well. Don't say "insomnia" when you can say "can't get to sleep" or "can't stay asleep."

Straightforward - If you can get your message across without using adjectives, leave them out because it makes your copy more direct, but be sure to use an adjective when necessary! When the adjective describes your competitive point of difference or your unique brand value, include it.

- Use active verbs and get to the point.

- Cut your introduction and jump right into the meat of the story.

- Eliminate irrelevant information.

- Avoid qualifiers that weaken the impact of your information. These "weasel words" include "might," "could," "possible," "probable," "perhaps" and "strive." Instead, use words like "will" and "can" to describe the results your product or service will provide for the customer.

Selective - Speak the same language as your customers. Use the words they use to describe themselves and their problems or needs. Avoid jargon, but utilize key words that will give a clue to your audience that you "get it" or "get them."

CONCISE

You only have a few seconds to get your customer's attention. Use as few words as possible to convey your message, and make sure they are the right words! Marketing guru Seth Godin says that "if you can't state your position in 8 words or less, you don't have a position." **Make it concise!** Here are some simple tips:

- Keep your sentences fewer than 15 words

- Break up any longer sentences with ellipses or dashes

- Use bulleted lists

- Keep paragraphs between 2-4 sentences (6 at the absolute maximum)

- Know it's all right to throw in some one- or two-word paragraphs.

- Take a breath – on paper, web or in person.

When we think of concise and persuasive copy, we often think of slogans or tag lines – and they work, provided they are focused on what you are selling. I can think, for example, of two competing 3-word slogans, each appealing to a different segment of their target market: Hertz – We're # 1; Avis – We Try Harder. Only three words each, yet they told the whole story!

COMPELLING

Finally, your copy should move your customer to action. Make the customer know that they MUST HAVE what you are offering! Remember that you are selling results, not products or services – make those results come alive in your customer's mind. Make it compelling!

- Use feeling words - Feeling words evoke emotion in your audience and help to paint the picture of what life will be like once they use your product or service.

- Use sensory descriptions – Talk about what your customers will see, hear, feel, touch and taste in order to engage them in your message.

- Paint the picture of difference – Create a clear contrast between what your customers are experiencing now and what they will experience after they use your product or service. Another option is to describe an intensification of the pain that the customers are currently experiencing – that's what life will be like if they *don't* buy from you.

- Use superlatives – Using words like "biggest," "best," "most" can spur your customer to action by increasing their desire for your product or service.

Think about the most powerful piece of copy you can remember. It probably meets all of these criteria. The one that comes to my mind is FedEx® – When it absolutely, positively has to be there overnight.® No question about what they are selling or why I need it!

Chapter Three

Keys to Supercharging Your Copy

Your selling power is directly related to the power of your copy. Even the best product or service cannot sell itself. Here are the keys to supercharging your sales copy:

Focus on the Customer

Your copy should be focused on your customers. Talk about their problems, their needs, and the solutions that will work for them. Then, tell them why YOU are the right choice to bring them the results they want. Good sales copy is like a good conversation. People want to know that you understand them – that you "get it." When people feel understood, they feel valued and a relationship is established. Remember, it's not about you, it's about them!

- Use first person and write as though you were having a one-to-one conversation.

- Relate personal experience by using phrases such as "when I," "we," or "people like us."

- Normalize their experience by connecting them to others.

🔑 Talk Benefits First, Then Features

Tell your ideal customers how their businesses or their lives will change after working with you or buying your product. Put yourself in the shoes of the person reading your copy. Their first question is, *"What's in it for me?"* You have to address that question, and you've got to stress the benefits of your product or service. What will they have more of? What will they have less of? How will they feel better or different? The bigger the change you promise, the more likely they are to buy. Be honest and describe the best success scenario you can offer. Once you have described the benefits, tell them HOW you'll provide what they need. Provide credible proof to support your promise of benefits. Benefits and features go hand in hand and your customer needs to know both in order to make a decision.

🔑 Make It Memorable

Whether your copy is online or in print, you need to make it stick in your customers' minds. External "noise" competes with your message. Here are some ways to make your message memorable:

- Leave visual clues – use bold type or bullets to draw attention to key points.

- Break it into chunks – think 5 Keys, 3 Steps, 7 Secrets.

- Make it musical – alliteration and rhythm stick in the brain.

- Provide a "hook" - use a title or tagline that resonates in the brain.

Write Like You Speak

Are you perfectly comfortable talking about your business in conversations or from the podium, yet get uncomfortable when you're faced with a blank page or computer screen? Don't let all of that white space intimidate you! The truth is that sales copy is just a conversation on paper. Imagine that you are talking to just one person -- your ideal customer. Write your copy as if you were recording that discussion. Write a bit and then stop and think about how your prospect would respond. When you hear that response in your head, then write the words you'd say next. Conversation marketing is very popular right now and if you can master the art of creating conversational copy, you'll be right on trend.

Keep the Customer Interested

If the copy feels long to you, chances are it feels long to the customer, too. Use graphics, photographs, audio and video to break up text. Say or do something unexpected or funny. The point is to keep them engaged long enough to get them to say *yes*.

Provide Proof

Whatever you are trying to sell or promote, offer proof that it works. Proof can include testimonials, photos, screen shots, research and statistics.

Keep It Honest

Don't make wild claims just to get business. Build a good reputation by being up front and honest with your potential customers. In addition to appreciating your honesty, they will recommend you to others as a business owner who is true to your word and claims.

Language Tips and Tricks

Here are some basic tips for skillful use of language that will keep your copy strong and powerful. While content is key, careful craft with language can change good copy into great copy.

Avoid Wimpy Verbs

Wimpy verbs such as "be" and "is" occupy space without adding meaning. So instead of "There is one simple omission that can transform a sentence from boring to brilliant," write "One simple omission can transform a sentence from boring to brilliant."

End a Series with the Longest Item

Begin with the shortest item and work toward the longest or most complex to avoid confusion and create a more rhythmic sentence. If you have a series like "He was always early for dinner, quiet and boring," opt for "He was quiet, boring and always early for dinner."

Avoid Weasel Words

Unless you are legally obligated to include qualifying language, leave out mushy modifiers such as "several," "nearly," "approximately" or "almost." Specifics tell your audience that you know what your product can do based on tests, research, results, etc.

Modify Thy Neighbor

Neighboring clause that is. Make sure your modifiers apply directly to the pertinent clause in question. Do this and you'll avoid such mistakes as "I tripped over an ottoman running through the living room." (The ottoman wasn't running through the living room, you were.)

Use Single Verbs to Avoid Doublespeak

Don't use two verbs when one will do. "The computer was operating and running smoothly" reads better as "The computer was running smoothly." Instead of "He was hungry and ran out of energy," go for the more direct "He ran out of energy."

Vary Sentence Length

In conversation, it is natural to vary the length of your sentences. Sentences in written copy should also vary in length. This variety in pace and rhythm keeps the reader interested.

Go Short and Sweet

Use the shortest phrase possible to convey your meaning. Why use a 4- to 5-word phrase when a 1- to 2-word version will do nicely—with no loss in meaning? Instead of "in view of the fact that" use "since" or "because." Word economy is particularly important when space is at a premium.

Don't Overstate the Obvious

Clear writing avoids redundancy. Phrases like "anticipate in advance," "totally finished," or "vital essentials" can be simplified to "anticipate," "finished," and "essentials."

The primary objective of copy, regardless of medium, is to create an effective message that resonates with the target audience. This golden rule applies to websites, brochures, speeches, and sales letters. Compelling copy is the secret super power that will get you super results.

If the headline is a good one, it is a relatively simple matter to write the copy.
~ John Caples

Chapter Four

Making a U-Turn with Headlines

There's no doubt about it. Headlines are the most important part of your copy. After all, if your headline doesn't grab the customer, the rest of the copy doesn't matter! Your headline either "grabs" prospects by the jugular... or it doesn't. If the headline fails, nothing else matters because the rest of your copy never even gets a fair reading. Your copy is competing with about 5,000 other advertising messages every day, and your customer needs to do something to narrow the field in the battle for time and attention. A strong headline assures that you will make the cut.

According to *Copyblogger*, 80% of the people who get your message will read your headline – but only 20% will go on to read further. So you must take the time to make your headlines the best they can be. When you think of it in monetary terms, once you have written a successful headline, you have earned 80 cents out of your dollar. Little things mean a lot when it comes to headlines. One recent study conducted by Content Marketing Institute found that including a hyphen or colon in the headline increased the click-through rate by 9% over headlines without either.

Headlines fail when they don't match the article written or aren't relevant to a specific theme. Don't make the customer think too hard about why you chose a particular headline. Headlines should do their job of attracting the customer and drawing them into the body of your copy. If the customer lingers too long with the headline they may not get to the heart of the matter (the call to action) before they move on to the next item of interest.

The 50/50 Rule of Headlines

Many copywriting gurus suggest that you should spend half of the time it takes you to write an entire piece of sales copy on the headline. While the rule is not hard and fast and no copy monitor will be grading you, it's a great guideline. Think of it as a case of improving the odds. If 80% of people who see your message will read the headline and 20% will read further – where do you need to focus to boost your results? If your headline could grab 85% of your readers and it were powerful enough to get 25% of those people to read further, you are powerfully boosting your results. Here's the math:

For 100 Readers – Average Headline - 80 read headline; 16 read further

For 100 Readers – Power Headline – 85 read headline; 21 read further.

U-Turn Ahead

The headline is your traffic signal, the sign that points the way to your product or service. Sometimes it takes making a U-Turn to get yourself going in the right direction. So, how do you create headlines that make customers make a U-Turn right into your sales funnel? Michael Masterson suggests that powerful headlines follow the 4 U Formula. They signal that your product, service or offer is:

- Urgent – you are offering something vital, time-limited, limited in quantity

- Unique – what you offer is one of a kind; can't miss

- Useful – what you offer is practical; a tool, tip or tactic

- Ultra-specific – you offer something unique and tailor-made for your audience.

Conveying Urgency

People have a natural tendency to resist change and avoid making decisions. Without a strong force to persuade them to act, they are likely to stick with the status quo – which means they are unlikely to make a purchase. A sense of urgency in your headline can be that persuasive force. Everybody wants to belong and nobody wants to lose out. If you persuade your customers that immediate action is essential, they will take the time to read further. Not everyone will buy, but at least they will have considered your proposition.

Scarcity and urgency are two powerful copy elements that usually go together to produce outstanding results. A good example of this concept is the combination of the counter and time left indicators on home shopping television shows. As the counter goes up and the timer counts down, the sense of urgency increases. Express urgency with words that have an implied or specific negative result from failure to act: "can't afford," "Don't miss out," "mistake," "fail", "left behind," "limited," "only."

Using Uniqueness

Writing a unique headline doesn't mean you have to re-invent the wheel. When you find a compelling headline, follow the form and make it unique for your audience. Both your headline itself and your offer must be "one of a kind" to maximize the uniqueness strategy. One way to see if your headline is unique is to plug it into Google and enclose it in double quotation marks. If the search doesn't bring back exact results, the headline itself is unique.

It's also important to show through the headline that your product or content is unique. Here are some words that convey uniqueness: "one of a kind," "only," "special," and "exclusive."

Making It Useful

We all know that people are reading copy because they are looking for something. Martha Hanlon of Wide Awake Business says everybody wants a pill – the question is whether they want a vitamin or an aspirin. A vitamin is for customers who are motivated to buy based on pleasure – they want MORE of a good thing. The aspirin is for the clients who are motivated to buy to relieve their pain – they want LESS of a bad thing.

Headlines that point the way to something useful show that you are offering something that people can consume quickly, use immediately and get results easily. Some of the key words you can include in your headlines to signal that your content is useful are:

- Tips
- Reasons
- Lessons
- Tricks
- Ideas
- Ways
- Principles
- Facts
- Templates
- Secrets
- Strategies

Making It Ultra-Specific

Assume that your prospects know very little about your products. They will have many questions. An ultra-specific headline will answer enough of those questions to keep them engaged in the conversation with you, either by reading more of the copy or by making a purchase. Chances are you have competitors selling something similar to the very people you are targeting. Get ahead of your competitors by specifically telling customers what they have to gain—and lose—from you right up front.

When you are ultra-specific with your headline, you convey more certainty and authority. Both of these qualities are persuasive to potential customers. Headlines that are ultra-specific give the reader a sense of what they can expect as they click to read the content.

Don't confuse your readers with your headline. Avoid vagueness. Get straight to the point. Use specific numbers and data. The brain is naturally receptive to numbers because they help to organize things in our minds. The brain seems to believe and be more receptive to odd numbers. Some studies suggest that the headline accounts for up to 50% of the effectiveness of a blog post and that headlines with numbers tend to generate 73% more social shares and engagement. Leave behind the vague promises that everyone else is making. Attract customers' curiosities with headlines full of concrete facts and figures. For example, don't just say "increase profits," say "increase profits by thousands of dollars." By adding this tiny detail, you immediately change from a generic headline to an enticing offer.

Five Approaches to Headlines

Keeping in mind the four U's, there are five approaches to writing the headline and crafting the psychological appeal of your copy. Each has its own power depending upon the needs and motivations of your ideal customer. Consider these examples of headlines focused on lead generation:

- **State a powerful benefit** - "Double Your Leads, Quadruple Your Profits"

- **Pique curiosity** - "7 Secrets to Lead Generation"

- **Report breaking news** - "New Formula for Lead Generation Doubles Results"

- **Offer immediate gratification** - "Get 10 New Leads Today"

- **Ask a question** – "How Many Leads Are You Losing?"

Each of these headlines could be used for the same content about generating leads. Each has a slightly different appeal and a master at messaging would choose just the right one to appeal to the target customer. Over time, you will learn which headline style works best with your customers. Use that approach the majority of the time, but don't be afraid to change things occasionally just to keep things interesting. Shifting approaches from time to time does two things: it allows you to capture new leads who weren't responsive to your standard approach and it keeps your ongoing customers interested by offering them something new.

Too many important details? Consider adding a sub-headline. The real headline should include the most captivating points, and a sub-headline can add information to seal the deal. When the headline and sub-headline are positioned close together, many customers can be enticed into reading both sentences right off the bat!

Word Choice

The psychology and focus of the headline is very important. Think about specific word choice as well. Positives work better than negatives, so keep your headlines positive, upbeat, and full of inspiration. By the time prospects get to the end of that very first line, they should not only want to keep reading—they should be eager and excited to keep reading!

Incorporating industry-specific words in your headline lets your customers know that they are in the right place and that you are "one of them." Don't use words that are taboo or out of favor with your target market. If you have done a good job at getting very specific with your niche, your word choices will be easier to make. Trying to find a word that resonates with everyone all the time is an almost impossible task.

Blogger David Crowther suggests that word choice can do a few things for your headlines: stimulate intrigue, create drama or raise doubts. Stimulating intrigue is creating temptation for your customer. Entice your customer with adjectives such as "extraordinary," "fascinating," "amazing" and "awesome." Grab their attention, and make further engagement more tempting. When you want to create drama, use very intense words such as "kill," "fear," "dark" or "death" to create a sense of urgency and importance. Sure, it might be melodramatic to talk about the "death of copywriting as we know it" (insert your own industry here), but for creating highly shareable, attention-grabbing headlines, this method works. In a similar vein, use negative words such as "no," "stop" and "without" to tap into people's insecurities. "10 habits you should start" is weaker than "10 habits you should stop."

Of course, there is one magic word that makes headlines particularly compelling. Care to take a guess? The word is **YOU.** Using this word is a clear signal to the customer that you understand it is all about them – and they like that! The headline is your first and best chance to establish your relationship with the customer and using the word "you" sends a signal that the customer is the most important party in that relationship.

Four Key Elements

By the end of your headline, the customer should know what they stand to gain, how easily they can benefit, and how fast they can start benefiting! Touch on as much of the following as you can:

- What your product is – "an e-book," "a technique"

- How it's used – "right from your browser," "effortlessly"

- What's required to use it – "less than two minutes of your time"

- Benefits from using it – "increases profits," "doubles memory"

Writing a great headline doesn't guarantee the success of your sale. The benefit conveyed in the headline still needs to be properly satisfied in the body copy, either with your content or your offer. However, failing to write a great headline means you may never get the chance to make the sale.

Critical Questions

Clayton Makepeace of *Early to Rise eZine* provides a list of six critical questions to ask yourself when working to create your most powerful headline:

1. Does your headline offer the reader a reward for reading?

2. What specifics could you add to make your headline more intriguing and believable?

3. Does your headline trigger a strong, actionable emotion the reader already has about the subject at hand?

4. Does your headline present a proposition that will instantly get your prospect nodding his or her head?

5. Could your headline benefit from the inclusion of a proposed transaction?

6. Could you add an element of intrigue to drive the prospect into your opening copy?

Create Your Own Headline Builder

You will always be writing headlines, so it's a worthwhile investment of your time to build a library of headline structures, words and approaches that work for you. Make a list of 20 words that describe the benefits of your product or service. Create a "clip file" of headlines that particularly captured your attention so that you can use them as models for your own powerful headlines. What are the ways that you can pique interest, create drama, or demonstrate urgency? What are the ways that describe your uniqueness? Having these words at the ready will help to ensure that your headlines grab attention and keep people reading.

Chapter Five

The Power of Brand Positioning

Let's be honest. You are probably not the first or the only person to offer your product or service. In many cases, you are just one face in a very crowded picture. Don't be discouraged, though. The good news is that *you are the only one* that does it exactly the way you do it. And, for your ideal customer – that's exactly what they are looking for!

The **Brand Positioning Statement** is the statement that tells you WHY your customers should choose you and what sets you apart from all the others. Sometimes, people confuse a brand positioning statement with the "elevator speech." That's the response that you offer when someone asks, "What do you do?" or "What is your business?" A brand positioning statement is a more specific description of your business identity – and it may be used later in the process of developing a relationship with your potential customer. Often, the brand positioning statement is considered the INTERNAL document that guides and frames your EXTERNAL communication.

If the elevator speech gets someone interested in the type of service you provide or the type of product you sell, the brand positioning statement tells someone (maybe you) why they should purchase your service or product rather than your competitors'. A clear statement of your brand shines the spotlight on you so your customers:

- See You FIRST
- See you CLEARLY
- See your VALUE
- See themselves saying YES!

Four Components to Brand Positioning

There are four major components to brand positioning. Taken together these four components develop your statement of brand positioning – the articulation of what you want you and your business to be known for. It is important to revisit these components as your business grows and changes and as you become more aware of what it is that motivates your customers. There are three specific times where it is essential to review these components: when you are starting your business, when your business is doing especially well and when your business is faltering.

Making sure you know where you are headed with your brand when you set out is a "no-brainer," but it is largely based on speculation and anticipation. Even if you have been in business before and done a stellar job of market research, no one else has **your** particular combination of skills, experience and expertise. Understanding how your unique combination of talents matches up with your customers' hopes, fears, dreams and distress requires a good analysis.

When your business is doing especially well, take a look at what's working. Examine which factors are critical to your success and must be maintained even as your business grows and changes and which things are not as essential. Replicating what works will save you lots of time as you develop new products and programs.

When your business is faltering, take a look at your brand positioning one more time. Where are you and your customer not in synch? Are you somehow missing the boat at conveying your particular value? Are you not setting yourself apart from the competition? As you make adjustments to bring the business to a stronger state, what can you let go of from your previous brand position and what must you keep?

Here are the four critical components that to consider every time you create or adjust your brand positioning:

1. Define your ideal customer in specific terms

2. Describe your customer's pain points

3. Compare without criticism

4. Paint a promising picture in describing benefits

Define Your Ideal Customer in Specific Terms

Everyone who has ever been through a business basics course has done the exercise of creating their ideal customer. Sometimes, this prototype is referred to as an avatar. There are many forms and templates out there that can help you to create this image. Your ideal customer is not imaginary – that person, perhaps hundreds and thousands like that person – exists and it is your job to know your ideal customers so thoroughly that you can find them in the vast sea of consumers.

One good way to do this is to think about "a day in their life" and how they would describe themselves. Think about a broad general category of people – say women – and think of that as 100% of the available possible customer pool. Your ideal customers are probably only 5-10% of that pool. They are women who have specific characteristics, pain points, connections, readiness, wants and needs.

There is a good way to know if you are getting specific enough in developing this vision of your ideal customer. Think of one of those classroom or workshop exercises where the instructor asks a series of questions. Every time you answer a question with *yes* – you stay standing. If you answer *no*, you sit down. When only a small number of people are still standing, you have identified your target group. In a sales presentation, this is when you'd say, "Congratulations! – my offer is for you." In your copy, you might say, "If you are 'x' and you are 'y' and you feel 'z', you need this product!" Each one of those "ands" is a place where the customers opt in or opt out of identifying themselves with what you have to offer.

Describe Your Customer's Pain Points

It's the Golden Rule of copywriting: "Know your target audience." It is impossible to persuade someone you know nothing about to take any type of action. So how, exactly, do you get to know your prospective customers? The simplest way is to ask them!

For copywriters, this task is an essential investment. When you must make a connection with someone you've never met, it can be frustrating. People buy products or services because they have a need. One of two motivations – toward pleasure or away from pain – will drive most customers. The vast majority of people are motivated to buy by moving away from pain. This is no surprise. If you think of a decision to buy as making a commitment to change, it is logical that people who are unhappy or uncomfortable are more highly motivated to change than those who are content. And even happy people are motivated to change if the offer is enticing enough.

In this age of popping a pill for everything, you need to decide if your customers want a vitamin or an aspirin. Those who want a vitamin are moving from happy or content to happier – they want more of a good thing. Those who want an aspirin are moving from pain to no pain. Your customer either wants MORE, LESS, BETTER or DIFFERENT. And, more specifically they want HOW THEY WILL FEEL WHEN THEY HAVE IT.

Here is where you describe what your customers want to do, think, say, have or feel differently after working with you. This can be getting rid of a negative or taking on a positive.

When you think about the pain point – think about what their current feelings cause them to do and provide a way for them to stop doing it.

For example, it isn't just that your customers feel stressed—it's that when they are stressed, they are more prone to making mistakes, snapping at people, forgetting things. Your job is to describe how your product will help them to avoid mistakes, treat people positively and remember things.

Compare Without Criticism

Identify the unique value your business brings. Write out what makes you unique in these four areas – skills, passion, talents and experiences. For products – think ease, effectiveness. Get clear on how these make you different from your competitors and more able to help a specific type of person with a specific problem or need. This is one place where comparison works to your advantage – if you are bigger, newer, faster, cheaper, more effective, less complicated – tell the customer that. But – here's what's important – do it WITHOUT criticism. NEVER name your competitor – and talk about your POSITIVES, rather than their NEGATIVES.

Of course, compare yourself to others on a factor that is important to your target audience! Help your customer to "connect the dots" that paint the picture that YOU are the solution to their problem.

Paint a Promising Picture of Life with Benefits

Define the outcomes or benefits you deliver. List the benefits your customers achieve from using your product or service. This isn't a list of features like "4 hours of design" or "3 dog training sessions," it's more about giving them an outcome they desire such as "a brand you'll love to promote" or "a dog that comes when called."

Here is where you describe what your customers will do, think, say, have or feel differently after working with you. This can be getting rid of a negative or taking on a positive. Think back to your customer's pain points. Are they buying toward pleasure or away from pain? This will tell you what picture you need to be painting in words in order to persuade them to act. For customers motivated toward pleasure, you will be developing the most positive, delightful picture possible. Think rainbows, sparkles and upbeat music. On the other hand, for customers motivated to buy away from pain, you may need to paint the picture of what it will be like if they **don't** purchase your product or service. Think dark clouds, gray or black instead of color, and ominous music. Of course, both you and the customer hope that one day they will be experiencing those rainbows and sparkles, but at this point, that may be too big a leap. You may need to

45

paint a picture for them in two parts – stopping the pain first and then acquiring the pleasure. Either way, this picture must be as vivid and detailed as possible. The customers must be able to imagine themselves inside the picture you are painting – starting to think, "That could be me." Once they believe it is possible, you have positioned yourself to move them to the buying decision, where they declare, "That **will** be me!"

How to Know if Your Brand Positioning Is Working

One you have created your brand position and built your business around it, how will you know if you have done a good job? There are some basic questions that you can ask yourself in order to make that assessment:

1. Does it identify my brand's unique value to my customers?

2. Does it produce a clear picture in my mind that's different from my competitors?

3. Is it focused on my ideal customers?

4. Is it memorable and motivating?

5. Is it consistent in all areas of my business?

6. Is it easy to understand?

7. Can anybody else make the same statement?

8. Is my brand promise believable and credible?

9. Will it help me make more effective marketing and branding decisions?

If you can answer *yes* to six or more of these questions, you have mastered the fundamentals of brand positioning. Now you just need to make some small tweaks in the areas where you are not quite hitting the mark. This adjustment may be comparatively minor – there is no need to go all the way back to square one.

See if you can find clues about what needs to be adjusted based on where people drop out of the decision to buy. If it is early, perhaps you do not have a clear picture of your ideal customer. It may be either too broad or too narrow, or it may be poorly described. Think about those "if this...and this..." questions or statements you are putting forth. Where are you hitting the bulls eye and where are you missing the mark? If the customer drops out further along in the process – perhaps when you think the customer is 90% there – you might want to re-think how you are painting the picture of benefits. Are you too rosy or too dark? Not detailed enough? Not believable? Examining these questions will help you to re-tool your brand positioning until it is a perfect fit for your ideal customer.

Measuring Your Brand Positioning

If you are more analytical than intuitive, it is important to know how to measure if you've properly positioned yourself. Positive trends in these indicators are reflections of effective brand positioning:

- Increased sales

- Response and recognition within your industry

- High percentage of returning customers

- Increase in market share

- Internal consistency across products, services and people.

Powerful and precise brand positioning can set you apart from the many others who have similar products and services and ensure that you are not just a face in the crowd, but the Leader of the Pack!

Chapter Six

Making Your Case

Are Keywords the Real Key?

Many copywriters make the mistake of writing only for search engine optimization (SEO) without regard to the other elements of creating compelling copy. Just stringing the right key words together may be enough to get you noticed, but it is not good enough to engage customers to the point of purchasing your product or service. Copywriting is more about your human customers and prospects than it is about search engines and algorithms. In fact, the concept of keywords focuses on identifying what will attract and keep the customer's attention as they move toward and respond to your call to action. If you want truly effective SEO copy, you'll take time to learn that keyword use goes beyond the search engines.

Keywords began with searches initiated by consumers. Compiling information about millions of such searches led to the identification of keywords related to specific topics. The same holds true today. Keywords don't just appear out of nowhere. There are specific services and programs that compile information about the exact phrases human beings are typing to Google, Yahoo!, and other engines. When your website copy includes those words and phrases, you're doing more than boosting your rankings; you're also helping to steer the site visitor from the search engine to the right page of your site.

Don't make the mistake of over-generalizing your copy in an attempt to broaden your audience and please everyone at once. Even when you have identified a small, clear niche of ideal customers, there are variations within that group that make one offer or program more appealing to some than to others. And, of course, being human, your customers grow, and change their minds over time. When you write copy for a clearly defined customer you refer to as "you," rather than "many people," or "our customers," the person for whom you are writing will recognize that your copy is directed to them. This is one of the most effective strategies in copywriting for the web.

There are mixed opinions on the relative merits of a short sales piece with lots of white space versus long and detailed copy. The long and short of the debate is this...what type of buyer are you targeting—impulsive or analytical?

The Impulsive Buyer

This is the person who makes decisions and takes action quickly. He'll skim the headlines and subtopics, glance at the photos and captions, and make a snap decision. Attention-getting headlines and sub-headers, visual appeal through graphics, photos, fonts and color persuade these buyers. Short copy works best for impulsive buyers.

The Analytical Buyer

This group of buyers believes that the proof is in the details. They'll read everything including the fine print. For analytical buyers, use the strategies that you employ for the impulsive buyer and then add the detail and logical explanations the analytic buyer needs under the proper heading, and you've got a winning marketing piece that is guaranteed to be successful.

Successful copy will address the needs of both types of buyers, regardless of length. Let's look at what you need to do to reach buyers. Inside knowledge of how your potential buyers react is the key to getting their attention... and boosting your sales results.

The Hidden Conversation

Your marketing copy is one side of a conversation. The other side of the conversation is occurring inside the customer or potential customer's brain. Think of that hidden conversation as a series of questions that your sales copy must answer, either explicitly or implicitly. The hidden conversation will contain some combination of these statements and questions:

- Do you know what I want most from you? If you don't, don't bother.

- What do you do? How will it help me? What's in it for me?

- Why should I believe you?

- Why should I listen to you?

- Is it easy for me to read, understand, navigate, and "scan" your marketing material?

- Are you a specialized expert in your field for my situation or my needs or my type of business?

- Don't bore me!

- I want ALL the details. Give me product information, product applications, CAD drawings and plans, costs and shipping. Talk to me person to person, and not from some emotionless corporation.

- I make purchases based on my emotions, but I won't admit that.

- Will you save me time or money? I'm in!

- Make it easy for me to take action No fluff, please.

-

- I'm a comparison shopper. Give me details before I buy.

- Be specific; generalities go right into my garbage.

- What's your guarantee?

- I don't like taking risks. Can I test your product, service or company first, in a low or no cost way, before I make a large commitment?

- Give me ammunition to justify the investment to my boss on an ROI basis.

When you are effective in conducting this "hidden conversation, you will be a sales superstar.

The "You" Point of View

When you have found your mission and created a business based on your passion and personal experience, it is easy to make your sales story all about you. Your weight-loss story might be admirable, but what does it mean to your customer or prospect? Talking mostly about yourself is a turnoff. Talk to your customer about something important in her life and you've got her undivided attention. Hold that attention as long as possible as you urge the customer toward the decision point.

More buying decisions are based on emotions than on logic. When you discover the emotional triggers for your ideal customer, you can describe everything through that person's eyes.

Remember the old marketing phrase "What's in it for me?" You need to answer this question in every part of your copy from the headline to the call to action. Your customers will only make a purchase when the benefit to them is clear and compelling. Also, you need to make a stronger benefit case than your competitors to make the sale.

Buying decisions often rely on emotion rather than on logic. If only there were a simple checklist that captured everything that your customer is thinking! Your job is creating that checklist in your mind. You might even want to put it down on paper. Filter all of your copy through this frame of reference. The connection between your customer's problem and your solution should be clear every step of the way. The minute you stray from your customer's point of view is the minute in which you can lose the sale.

Establishing Trust

Customers buy from people that they know, like, and trust. Your copy must present you as credible and trustworthy as well as make the case that your product or service is reliable and effective. Build credibility with your customers by:

- Providing testimonials

- Invoking authority from others
- Being honest and authentic.

It's a challenge to get people to trust what you say, particularly at the beginning of your business relationship. You can be honest, trustworthy and reliable, but that is not enough. Your customers need to see and feel that honesty and integrity. The style and content of your copy set the tone for how your customers perceive you. In this case, having others to make your case, either through testimonials by satisfied customers or endorsements from trusted authorities, will make the case more easily than making those assertions yourself.

Guarantee your work. If you are willing to stand behind your work 100%, this tells the customer that there is little risk involved in doing business with you. Trust flourishes in the absence of risk. Make sure that your guarantee is prominent and visible in your copy and honor the guarantee when requested. It should be rare that a customer asks for a refund or other provisions of a guarantee, but when it occurs, make the situation right promptly and gracefully. The stronger your guarantee, the more trust it inspires.

Appearances Matter

Large blocks of text without sufficient white space or other visuals can be intimidating to your customer. Use short paragraphs and sub-headings, even in shorter copy such as emails and flyers. Break some of the standard rules for formal written communication by using asterisks, dashes and ellipses to break up the copy and give it the rhythm of speech. Bulleted lists provide both emphasis and visual relief. Use them liberally throughout your sales copy. Think of your bullet points as mini-headlines. Each one is another chance for your customer to say "yes." All of these small "yesses" build up to the final "yes" that comes with purchase.

Educate, Then Persuade

It might be necessary to educate your customers before persuading them. You can't assume that customers are as familiar with your business as you are. Customers must have a certain level of knowledge and understanding about the business to make an informed decision about the value of your product or service. When customers do not understand value, they may have some resistance about price. If you jump right into persuading without even a little bit of education, you risk leaving the customer behind.

One good way to educate customers is through offering high-value content without an "ask" attached. Over time, potential customers become acquainted with you and your industry without feeling pressured to buy before they are ready. Remember that keeping customers is more cost-effective than getting new customers, so taking the time to invest in education will pay off in the long run.

Chapter Seven

Creating an Irresistible Call to Action

The Call to Action is the bookend to your headline – it's the place where the client accepts the offer or promise you made in the headline by making a commitment to connect with you either through signing up for your list or becoming an actual customer and BUYING what you have to offer.

All sales copy should include a call to action. Remember the "ABC" of selling: **A**lways **B**e **C**losing. People need direction. If you want them to make a purchase, you have to ask for the sale. Sometimes the call to action appears first in the headline, is repeated at least once through the body of the message and then again at the end of the message. Words like "Act Now," Limited Time Offer," or "Limited Supply" will urge your readers to contact you sooner rather than later.

It's amazing how many businesses don't ask explicitly for the sale. Their copy may spend so much time and space describing benefits and features that the writer assumes that the customer who has read the entire message is prepared to buy. But the simple truth is that you lose up to 20% of sales due to failure to include a call to action. A call to action does not always need to include a purchase. Many businesses start by offering a free product known as a lead magnet or opt-in. This practice is a popular method for building an email list through a low-to-no-risk offer. In this case, what you are asking for is the customer's email address. In some cases, more information such as physical address and phone number is required.

Whether you are asking for money or information, tell the customers exactly what you want them to do and when you want them to do it. (Now is best; before a specific time is next). Include the link, with a graphic or icon if possible, that gives specific directions. If it is appropriate, tell the customers what they will receive when they follow your directions and make the click. For example: "Click Here to Get Your Free Download" or "Click Here to Register."

It might seem obvious that you want people to make a purchase, especially after you have done a masterful job of making your case. Don't leave the customer hanging after you have made a compelling case for your business. If you do, you lose not only the current sale but future sales as well. Your specific call to action will ensure that this doesn't happen. With catalog style websites and lead pages, provide multiple opportunities to take action.

A Word About Websites

There are some specific things to consider when creating sales copy for websites, especially if you have a catalog-style or short copy site. First, offer multiple opportunities for the customer to buy your product or service. Once is not enough! If your site has multiple pages, there should be at least one call to action on every page. The call to action may always be a link to your order form or shopping cart. In addition to the "click" button, the call to action should include urgency-building action phrases such as:

- "Buy today!"
- "Limited time offer – get yours now!"
- "What are you waiting for?"
- "Click this link to order your own... "
- "Get started today, just click here!"
- "YES! I want to order now."

A word of warning – don't jump the gun by placing references to "buying" in the top fold of your website. That's the portion of the page that shows on the screen when the home page or landing page appears. Simply put, that placement is a case of too much, too soon – too much pressure before the customer has enough information to make a decision.

The only call to action that should appear in the top fold of your website is your Opt-In – otherwise known as a lead magnet or incredible free offer. It's the place where people buy-in by providing their e-mail address and you give them a little something in return. The old saying that "timing is everything" applies here and the timing is represented by the actual placement of the call to action.

Call Me Irresistible

Once your headline grabs your customers' attention and your unique brand position has convinced them that you have what they want, you need to move them to ACTION – to commit to creating a business relationship with you by joining your "tribe" or buying your product or service.

This is the crucial part of your sales copy. Your offer should be compelling, irrefutable and urgent. You want your reader to say, "This is a great offer. I've got nothing to lose but my problem." If you can, combine the big 3 in your offer – irresistible price, great terms, and a free gift. For example, if you're selling a cordless electric mower, your offer might be a discounted retail price, low interest rate, and a blade-sharpening tool. Raise the perceived value of your offer by adding on products or services – for electric mowers, it might be an extended warranty or safety goggles. Augment this with compelling benefits these additional products or services will provide.

Asking for the sale is simple, and the impact it can have on your bottom line is huge. By adding a simple call to action, you make it easy for your customers to understand what they're supposed to do. And once they know they're supposed to buy something from you, they will – and your profits will shoot through the roof!

5 Keys to Creating an Irresistible Call to Action:

Be direct – Don't leave the customers guessing about what they need to do to get what you have to offer. Some examples of direct language include; "get started," "sign up," "connect," "subscribe," or "download."

Use actionable language – Strong verbs give the client specific instructions on what to do – call, click, download, etc.

Be urgent - Your call to action should create urgency by conveying a message that your prospects are missing a great opportunity if they don't act right away. Convince them that the clock is ticking and delaying would result in missing the opportunity. Using words like "today," "now," or "immediately" can work wonders here by adding a sense of urgency.

Make it easy - The transition from call to action to performing the task must be seamless. A complicated call to action is bound to fail. For example, if you want your prospective customers to call, provide your phone number. Also, if you are offering something free of charge, such as a free demo or a free sample, don't forget to mention that in your call to action.

🔑**Be generous** - The key to getting customers to respond to your offers is to make them irresistibly generous. Can you afford to knock several dollars off the fee for your product or service? Or maybe you can make a strong guarantee, making your product or service almost risk free. Transferring the risk from the customer to you will help remove resistance to your offer.

In summary, make your offer irresistible. Make it worth the effort to the customer to place the order. Transfer the risk from the customer to you and add a sense of urgency. Then be sure to live up to what you have written in your copy. If you do these things, you'll see your sales skyrocket!

Chapter Eight

Pulling It All Together

Never underestimate the power of words. When you have the skill of creating compelling copy and combine it with the skill you have in performing the work that you do, you are creating a unique and powerful business proposition. Your sales copy gives your customer a "sneak peek" into working with you, so be sure that you include some actual content with all of the persuasion and selling.

Including "free information" helps to establish goodwill with the potential customer. It shows that you are generous and helps to develop a relationship. Even if prospects don't buy, they walk away with something valuable. It also helps to establish your credibility. This is an opportunity for you to show that you know your stuff. The substance you include in sales copy acts as a teaser. It's obvious that you are not saying everything you know and that there is a "lot more where that came from." In other words, if you are willing to give away this information you must have a lot more "secrets" up your sleeve.

Sales copy that includes education and actual content is referred to as "value-added." Providing such value is a win-win proposition: it gives something to the customer right up front and it lowers the sales resistance of the reader because you are in the giving rather than the taking mode. There is really no argument against someone who is giving you something for free. It provides a natural incentive for the prospect to read your entire sales letter. Any device that encourages readership will also improve sales, especially with longer sales copy. This technique of value-added copywriting works very well in service-type industries. There are many services where you can "reveal" a lot without fear of losing your value to the customer.

Compelling sales copy is the key to engaging prospects and turning them into customers. Sales copy is effective when it does three basic things:

- Attracts attention with powerful headlines

- Affirms connection by stating the unique brand position

- Accelerates commitment with a strong call to action.

When you master all three of these elements, your sales copy will be more than compelling, it will be super-powered – and it will create super results!

Happy writing!

About the Author

Gail Dixon is a Speaker, Best Selling Author, Coach and Consultant with more than 30 years of professional communication experience. As the founder and President of Masterful Messaging, Gail specializes in guiding people to name, frame and claim the verbal expression of their brand identity and core messaging. Her extensive experience combined with her unique gift of listening between the lines positions Gail as the top expert and trusted authority for creating compelling and authentic brand and personal messaging. She is a certified public speaker through Women's Prosperity Network and serves as a coach in their community.

"Copy is a direct conversation with the consumer."
~ *Shirley Polykoff*

Appendix

IDEAL CUSTOMER PROFILE SHEET

BRAND POSITIONING TEMPLATES

IDEAL CUSTOMER PROFILE SHEET

Describe Your Ideal Customer

<u>WHO</u> will you be selling to?

An individual -

Describe the qualities and characteristics of your customer.

Age Range	
Gender	
Marital Status	
Career	
Education Level	
Location	
Affiliations	
Income	
Hobbies	
Spending Habits	
Key Motivation	
Clubs or Activities	
Eating/Health Habits	
Influenced By	

A business -

Direct access to the final decision maker? ___Yes ___No

Describe the qualities and characteristics of the business.

Industry	
# of Employees	
Revenue	
Location	
Market Share	
Corporate Values	
Budget Available	
Influencing Factors	
Stage of Business	
Key Competitors	
Brand Identity	
Buying Cycle	

Describe the specific problems or challenges that are faced by your customer. Use the words they use. Then list the solution or benefit you provide to solve the problem.

(What do they want, think, feel, do, have or say that they want to change? If a business, what results do they need to achieve and what do they need to get those results?)

Problem or Challenge	Benefit - Result of Buying from You

In general, is your ideal customer motivated…

____Toward pleasure   ____Away from pain

Make a list of words that your ideal client might use to describe what he or she needs or is looking for.

_____

_____

_____

_____

_____

What are the objections or questions that might stop or prevent your customer from buying? How would you address those objections?

Objections	Response to Objections

What other things do you know or need to know about your ideal customer?

_____

_____

_____

_____

_____

_____

BRAND POSITIONING TEMPLATES

TEMPLATE # 1

For _____

[insert Target Market/Ideal Client]

_____

[insert Business Name/Brand]

is the _____ that offers _____

[insert Unique Point of Difference]   [insert Benefit]

through _____

[insert specific service].

Example 1:

For <u>animal lovers/owners who have fur babies, not pets,</u> The Pet Spa is the home away from home without crates or kennels that offers you a <u>guilt-free vacation</u> through family-centered boarding for your <u>fur baby</u>!

Note: In this template, the customer's pain point is implied at two places – "fur babies, not pets" and "guilt-free vacations."

Example 2:

For <u>health conscious consumers who want to release extra weight,</u> Meal Replacement Magic is the <u>scientifically proven supplement</u> that offers <u>weight loss without worry</u> in <u>convenient, low-cost and delicious meal replacement drinks.</u>

TEMPLATE # 2

If you are:

• _____

(describe ideal client; can be more bullets)

And you are:

• _____

(describe customer's pain point(s))

We are the:

• _____

(describe unique point of difference)

That:

• _____

(describe promise/benefit result)

Example 1

If you are: a solo business owner in a service-oriented business

And you are: not getting clients as fast as you want to or getting the wrong clients

We are: the no-fail client generation system

That: gets you 30 ideal, high-paying clients in 30 days – Guaranteed!

Example 2

If you are: a frequent business traveler

And you are: tired of rushing to the dry cleaner between trips

We are: the only traveler's butler service

That: delivers your completely packed suitcase for your next trip when you get home from this one!

Gail Dixon

MASTERFUL
MESSAGING
HARNESSING THE POWER OF WORDS

To work with Gail to create Masterful Messages for your business or personal life,
Email her at: gail@masterfulmessaging.com

www.ingramcontent.com/pod-product-compliance
Lightning Source LLC
Chambersburg PA
CBHW050608210326
41521CB00008B/1161